Spring Harvest
Bible Workbook

WORSHIP

One True King

Jenny Baker

Series editor for thematic workbooks – Jeff Lucas

Authentic

Equipping the Church for action

11 10 09 08 07 06 05   7 6 5 4 3 2 1

First published in 2005 by Spring Harvest Publishing Division and Authentic Media
9 Holdom Avenue, Bletchley, Milton Keynes, Bucks, MK1 1QR, UK
and 129 Mobilization Drive, Waynesboro, GA 30830-4575, USA

www.authenticmedia.co.uk

British Library Cataloguing in Publication Data

A catalogue record for this book is available from the British Library

ISBN 1-85078-633-X

Typeset by Spring Harvest
Cover design by Diane Bainbridge
Print management by Adare Carwin
Printed and Bound by J. H. Haynes & Co. Ltd., Sparkford

CONTENTS

ABOUT THIS BOOK

This study book looks at worship: worship of the one true God in the context of idolatry and worship in exile, and is based on the first half of the book of Daniel – chapters 1 to 7. It follows the structure of the book which contains parallel stories – chapters 2 and 7 tell of prophetic dreams; chapters 3 and 6 give the stories of two miracles of divine deliverance and chapters 4 and 5 tell us about the judgement of two powerful pagan kings. The chapters of Daniel will therefore be studied in that order, enabling you to pick up key themes that run through these parallel stories.

This workbook is written primarily for use in a group situation, but can easily be used by individuals who want to study the life of Daniel. It can be used in a variety of contexts, so it is perhaps helpful to spell out the assumptions that we have made about the groups that will use it. These can have a variety of names – home groups, Bible study groups, cell groups – we've used housegroup as the generic term.

- The emphasis of the studies will be on the application of the Bible. Group members will not just learn facts, but will be encouraged to think: 'How does this apply to me? What change does it require of me? What incidents or situations in my life is this relevant to?'
- Housegroups can encourage honesty and make space for questions and doubts. The aim of the studies is not to find the 'right answer', but to help members understand the Bible by working through the questions. The Christian faith throws up paradoxes. Events in people's lives may make particular verses difficult to understand. The house group should be a safe place to express these concerns.
- Housegroups can give opportunities for deep friendships to develop. Group members will be encouraged to talk about their experiences, feelings, questions, hopes and fears. They will be able to offer one another pastoral support and to get involved in each other's lives.
- There is a difference between being a collection of individuals who happen to meet together every Wednesday and being an effective group who bounce ideas off each other, spark inspiration and creativity and pool their talents and resources to create solutions together and whose whole is definitely greater than the sum of its parts. The process of working through these studies will encourage healthy group dynamics.

Space is given for you to write answers, comments, questions and thoughts. This book will not tell you what to think, but it will help you discover the truth of God's word through thinking, discussing, praying and listening.

FOR GROUP MEMBERS

▶ You will get more out of the study if you spend some time during the week reading the passage and thinking about the questions. Make a note of anything you don't understand.

▶ Pray that God will help you to understand the passage and show you how to apply it. Pray for other members in the group too, that they will find the study helpful.

▶ Be willing to take part in the discussions. The leader of the group is not there as an expert with all the answers. They will want everyone to get involved and share their thoughts and opinions.

▶ However, don't dominate the group! If you are aware that you are saying a lot, make space for others to contribute. Be sensitive to other group members and aim to be encouraging. If you disagree with someone, say so but without putting down their contribution.

FOR INDIVIDUALS

▶ Although this book is written with a group in mind, it can also be easily used by individuals. You obviously won't be able to do the group activities suggested, but you can consider how you would answer the questions and write your thoughts in the space provided.

▶ You may find it helpful to talk to a prayer partner about what you have learnt, and ask them to pray for you as you try and apply what you are learning to your life.

The New International Version of the text is printed in the book. If you usually use a different version, then read from your own Bible as well.

INTRODUCTION TO WORSHIP

'How can we sing the Lord's song in a strange land?' asked the exiled psalmist (Ps. 137). The book of Daniel gives the answer to the question. Through a series of dramatic events, Daniel and his friends show that it is possible to be faithful to God in the middle of a pagan culture. Daniel has the wisdom to know when to make a stand for his faith, and when to go with the flow. He refuses to be coerced into worshipping false idols or to give up the worship of the God that he loves so much. Through the discipline and faithfulness of his ordinary day-to-day life, he finds the resources to cope with remarkable challenges to his faith. More importantly, he discovers that his God is the God of all creation, the God of all history and the God of all peoples.

Daniel remains true to God in his acts of formal worship, but his story also shows how there is more to worship than singing songs or speaking prayers of praise. His character and actions shout of the faithfulness and power of the God of Israel. In the same way, our lives can be lives of witness and worship, even in the smallest detail, telling the world of the goodness of our God. In the words of George Herbert, we can pray

> *Teach me, my God and King,*
> *In all things Thee to see,*
> *And what I do in any thing,*
> *To do it as for Thee*

Daniel's story is rooted in the sixth century before Christ, but it is relevant to us, in our own pressured and pluralist culture. How can we sing God's song in a land in which we are a minority? What does it mean to be God's people and to live a godly life? How can we remain faithful when all around us is changing? The unforgettable stories of this book show us what it means to 'sing God's song' when we are strangers in the land and how we can keep the faith in times of trial.

WORSHIP IN EXILE

Aim: To consider what it is like to live and worship in exile, and to compare that experience to our own lives

In the third year of the reign of Jehoiakim king of Judah, Nebuchadnezzar king of Babylon came to Jerusalem and besieged it. And the Lord delivered Jehoiakim king of Judah into his hand, along with some of the articles from the temple of God. These he carried off to the temple of his god in Babylonia and put in the treasure house of his god.

Then the king ordered Ashpenaz, chief of his court officials, to bring in some of the Israelites from the royal family and the nobility—young men without any physical defect, handsome, showing aptitude for every kind of learning, well informed, quick to understand, and qualified to serve in the king's palace. He was to teach them the language and literature of the Babylonians. The king assigned them a daily amount of food and wine from the king's table. They were to be trained for three years, and after that they were to enter the king's service.

Among these were some from Judah: Daniel, Hananiah, Mishael and Azariah. The chief official gave them new names: to Daniel, the name Belteshazzar; to Hananiah, Shadrach; to Mishael, Meshach; and to Azariah, Abednego.

But Daniel resolved not to defile himself with the royal food and wine, and he asked the chief official for permission not to defile himself in this way. Now God had caused the official to show favour and sympathy to Daniel, but the official told Daniel, "I am afraid of my lord the king, who has assigned your food and drink. Why should he see you looking worse than the other young men your age? The king would then have my head because of you."

Daniel then said to the guard whom the chief official had appointed over Daniel, Hananiah, Mishael and Azariah, "Please test your servants for ten days: Give us nothing but vegetables to eat and water to drink. Then compare our appearance with that of the young men who eat the royal food, and treat your servants in accordance with what you see." So he agreed to this and tested them for ten days.

At the end of the ten days they looked healthier and better nourished than any of the young men who ate the royal food. So the guard took away their choice food and the wine they were to drink and gave them vegetables instead.

To these four young men God gave knowledge and understanding of all kinds of literature and learning. And Daniel could understand visions and dreams of all kinds.

At the end of the time set by the king to bring them in, the chief official pre-sented them to Nebuchadnezzar. The king talked with them, and he found none equal to Daniel, Hananiah, Mishael and Azariah; so they entered the king's service. In every matter of wisdom and understanding about which the king questioned them, he found them ten times better than all the magicians and enchanters in his whole kingdom.

And Daniel remained there until the first year of King Cyrus.

Daniel 1

TO SET THE SCENE

Has anyone any experiences of visiting, living or working in a completely different culture? What did you enjoy? What did you miss? How did it feel to be immersed in a different world? What customs or different ways of doing things made an impression on you?

Read the passage together

ABOUT THE BOOK OF DANIEL

Daniel is a book of two halves.

▶ Chapters 1 to 7 contain the stories of a group of young Jewish men taken into exile from Jerusalem to Babylon in the sixth century BC.
▶ Chapters 8 to 12 contain Daniel's prophetic visions, recounting dramatic events that lead to the coming of God's kingdom.
▶ It is written partly in Hebrew (1:1 – 2:4a and 8–12) and partly in Aramaic (2:4b to 7:28).

There has been debate over the centuries about when the book of Daniel was written. Recent evangelical scholarship suggests that the early chapters of Daniel were probably written in the sixth century BC, while later chapters were probably compiled in the second century BC.

There is no doubt, however, about when the action in Daniel took place. The third year of Jehoiakim's reign (1:1) was around 605 BC. Daniel then served in Babylon for seventy years until 536 BC, which was probably the year that the first of the exiles were allowed to return to Jerusalem under Zerubabbel (Ezra 1:2,3).

Daniel has a reputation for being a difficult book. As well as the controversies over its origin, purpose, dating and authorship, the strange apocalyptic prophecies in the later chapters are not easy to understand. But we mustn't let that put us off making the most of this amazing book. Daniel has a great deal to teach us in the twenty-first century church as we seek to sing the Lord's song in a strange land – to worship, to live out our faith in a culture that does not acknowledge God as Lord and King.

1 The Israelites were taken from their own home into exile. What thoughts, feelings or images does the word 'exile' conjure up for you?

WHAT DOES
SEARCH
THE BIBLE SAY?
2 What was the real reason God allowed them to be taken into exile? What could they have done about it (Jer. 25:1–11)?

WHAT DOES
SEARCH
THE BIBLE SAY?
3 The Israelites had certain expectations of their relationship with God. Look at Genesis 17:8, which sums up the covenant that God made with Abraham and then with successive generations of his descendants. What three things does God promise? What impact would exile have had on them?

4 What is the significance of some articles from the Israelite temple being taken and put in the temple of Nebuchadnezzar's god?

5 What changed for Daniel and his friends when they went to live in Babylon? What did they lose through the experience?

6 Why do you think Daniel accepted the new name Belteshazzar, but rejected the king's food? See 4:8 for the significance of his name.

ENGAGING WITH
THE WORLD
7 Daniel and his friends must have longed to be back in Jerusalem. What kind of world do you long for? How would our governments, courts, communities, schools, public festivals and other areas be different if God were honoured publicly?

THE END OF CHRISTENDOM?

From around the eleventh century to the end of the twentieth century, the Christian faith dominated European society – dictating its beliefs and assumptions, influencing its politics and laws, shaping its art and architecture and being followed by most of its people. Christendom is the word used to describe this world where Christianity had become so established in the culture that matters of faith overlapped with matters of public life. Christians were in the majority; the voice of the church was given privileged status in public discourse and the wider culture was deeply influenced by faith and theology.

There are different views as to the effect that Christendom has had on the life of the church and society. But many theologians and commentators say that Christendom is now over or soon will be – that we are living in Post–Christendom. They point to the massive decline in church attendance, increasing calls for the separation of church and state, a plurality of faiths and worldviews competing for attention, and a lack of respect and authority given to the voice of the church.

8. Read the section on The end of Christendom? and this quote from Kenneth Leech.

> *As Christians enter the twenty-first century, they do so as exiles, strangers and pilgrims, aliens in a strange land. They will need to learn the strategies of survival, and to sing the songs of Zion in the midst of Babylon.*

Do you agree with these analyses? Explain your view.

HOW DOES THIS

APPLY TO ME?

9 How at home do you feel in the culture around you? Can you see any parallels between what Daniel and his friends faced and your situation? What differences are there?

WORSHIP

The book of Daniel has a bleak start. And yet God is still with the Israelites even though they may feel he is far away.

Read Psalm 13.

Pray for people that you know who feel God is far from them, using the structure of this psalm, being honest about what is happening to them and how they feel about it, but choosing to trust in God's goodness.

DURING THE WEEK

The psalmist asked 'How can we sing the songs of the LORD while in a foreign land?' (Ps. 137:4). As we study Daniel we will find the answer to that question. But for now, what are the 'songs' that the culture around you sings? What does our culture consider important? What does it value? What does it worship?

In the week, look out for real songs that sum up for you what the culture around you values. Bring them to next week's session.

Also, read Daniel chapters 1 to 7 to get an overview of the passages that you will be studying for the next few weeks. It won't take long and there are some great stories in there!

FOR FURTHER STUDY

Just before Jesus returned to heaven, the disciples asked him 'Lord, are you at this time going to restore the kingdom to Israel?' (Acts 1:6). They expected him to bring an end to their exile and for Jerusalem to be restored to its place at the heart of God's plan. What is Jesus' response? Look at the early chapters of Acts. What did the disciples go through instead of the restored kingdom they were expecting? What did that do for their faith?

COMMUNICATING GOD'S WORD

Aim: to consider how we can be a prophetic voice to the world around us, and call people to worship

In the second year of his reign, Nebuchadnezzar had dreams; his mind was troubled and he could not sleep. So the king summoned the magicians, enchanters, sorcerers and astrologers to tell him what he had dreamed. When they came in and stood before the king, he said to them, "I have had a dream that troubles me and I want to know what it means."

Then the astrologers answered the king in Aramaic, "O king, live for ever! Tell your servants the dream, and we will interpret it."

The king replied to the astrologers, "This is what I have firmly decided: If you do not tell me what my dream was and interpret it, I will have you cut into pieces and your houses turned into piles of rubble. But if you tell me the dream and explain it, you will receive from me gifts and rewards and great honour. So tell me the dream and interpret it for me."

Once more they replied, "Let the king tell his servants the dream, and we will interpret it."

Then the king answered, "I am certain that you are trying to gain time, because you realise that this is what I have firmly decided: If you do not tell me the dream, there is just one penalty for you. You have conspired to tell me misleading and wicked things, hoping the situation will change. So then, tell me the dream, and I will know that you can interpret it for me."

The astrologers answered the king, "There is not a man on earth who can do what the king asks! No king, however great and mighty, has ever asked such a thing of any magician or enchanter or astrologer. What the king asks is too difficult. No-one can reveal it to the king except the gods, and they do not live among men."

This made the king so angry and furious that he ordered the execution of all the wise men of Babylon. So the decree was issued to put the wise men to death, and men were sent to look for Daniel and his friends to put them to death.

When Arioch, the commander of the king's guard, had gone out to put to death the wise men of Babylon, Daniel spoke to him with wisdom and tact. He asked the king's officer, "Why did the king issue such a harsh decree?" Arioch then explained the matter to Daniel. At this, Daniel went in to the king and asked for time, so that he might interpret the dream for him.

Then Daniel returned to his house and explained the matter to his friends Hananiah, Mishael and Azariah. He urged them to plead for mercy from the God of heaven concerning this mystery, so that he and his friends might not be executed with the rest of the wise men of Babylon. During the night the mystery was revealed to Daniel in a vision. Then Daniel praised the God of heaven and said:

"Praise be to the name of God for ever and ever; wisdom and power are his.

He changes times and seasons; he sets up kings and deposes them. He gives wisdom to the wise and knowledge to the discerning.

He reveals deep and hidden things; he knows what lies in darkness, and light dwells with him.

I thank and praise you, O God of my fathers: You have given me wisdom and power, you have made known to me what we asked of you, you have made known to us the dream of the king.

Then Daniel went to Arioch, whom the king had appointed to execute the wise men of Babylon, and said to him, "Do not execute the wise men of Babylon. Take me to the king, and I will interpret his dream for him."

Arioch took Daniel to the king at once and said, "I have found a man among the exiles from Judah who can tell the king what his dream means."

The king asked Daniel (also called Belteshazzar), "Are you able to tell me what I saw in my dream and interpret it?"

Daniel replied, "No wise man, enchanter, magician or diviner can explain to the king the mystery he has asked about, but there is a God in heaven who reveals mysteries. He has shown King Nebuchadnezzar what will happen in days to come. Your dream and the visions that passed through your mind as you lay on your bed are these:

"As you were lying there, O king, your mind turned to things to come, and the revealer of mysteries showed you what is going to happen. As for me, this mystery has been revealed to me, not because I have greater wisdom than other living men, but so that you, O king, may know the interpretation and that you may understand what went through your mind.

"You looked, O king, and there before you stood a large statue—an enormous, dazzling statue, awesome in appearance. The head of the statue was made of pure gold, its chest and arms of silver, its belly and thighs of bronze, its legs of iron, its feet partly of iron and partly of baked clay. While you were watching, a rock was cut out, but not by human hands. It struck the statue on its feet of iron and clay and smashed them. Then the iron, the clay, the bronze, the silver and the gold were broken to pieces at the same time and became like chaff on a threshing-floor in the summer. The wind swept them away without leaving a trace. But the rock that struck the statue became a huge mountain and filled the whole earth.

"This was the dream, and now we will interpret it to the king. You, O king, are the king of kings. The God of heaven has given you dominion and power and might and glory; in your hands he has placed mankind and the beasts of the field and the birds of the air. Wherever they live, he has made you ruler over them all. You are that head of gold.

"After you, another kingdom will rise, inferior to yours. Next, a third kingdom, one of bronze, will rule over the whole earth. Finally, there will be a fourth kingdom, strong as iron—for iron breaks and smashes everything—and as iron breaks things to pieces, so it will crush and break all the others. Just as you saw that the feet and toes were partly of baked clay and partly of iron, so this will be a divided kingdom; yet it will have some of the strength of iron in it, even as you saw iron mixed with clay. As the toes were partly iron and partly clay, so this kingdom will be partly strong and partly brittle. And just as you saw the iron mixed with baked clay, so the people will be a mixture and will not remain united, any more than iron mixes with clay.

"In the time of those kings, the God of heaven will set up a kingdom that will never be destroyed, nor will it be left to another people. It will crush all those kingdoms and bring them to an end, but it will itself endure for ever. This is the meaning of the vision of the rock cut out of a mountain, but not by human hands—a rock that broke the iron, the bronze, the clay, the silver and the gold to pieces.

"The great God has shown the king what will take place in the future. The *dream is true and the interpretation is trustworthy."*

Then King Nebuchadnezzar fell prostrate before Daniel and paid him honour and ordered that an offering and incense be presented to him. The king said to Daniel, "Surely your God is the God of gods and the Lord of kings and a revealer of mysteries, for you were able to reveal this mystery."

Then the king placed Daniel in a high position and lavished many gifts on him. He made him ruler over the entire province of Babylon and placed him in charge of all its wise men. Moreover, at Daniel's request the king appointed Shadrach, Meshach and Abednego administrators over the province of Babylon, while Daniel himself remained at the royal court.

Daniel 2

TO SET THE SCENE
What are the three most recognised symbols across the globe, from the Third World to the developed West?

Read the passage together.

PROPHECY
The term prophecy can be used to describe a wide range of activities recorded in Scripture and experienced in the church. These can include:

▶ the personal – where dreams, visions, words and images are used to give direction and insight to a particular individual.
▶ the predictive – where themes and events in the future are brought alive in present experience.
▶ the political – where the plumb line of God's truth and justice is brought to bear on the political and social realities of the day.

---

1 What do you learn about Nebuchadnezzar from this passage?

2 When Nebuchadnezzar was troubled, he automatically turned to magicians and astrologers for a solution. Where do

people look for wisdom in our world? Share what you noticed during the week. How involved is God in those solutions? Should Christians look for wisdom in other places?

HOW DOES THIS
APPLY TO ME

3 Daniel acted as a prophet in this story – hearing God's word and communicating it clearly. What experience have you had of the written word of God being prophetic – bringing a clear, relevant word of hope to a situation in which you have been involved?

What about spoken prophecy – have you heard a direct word from God that has provided guidance and encouragement to you?

How did you respond?

4 Worship is all that we offer to God, our whole lives, and how they reflect his grace to us. In what sense does this chapter present Daniel's life as a life of worship

▶ in his dealings with Arioch and his friends?
▶ in his response to the dream?
▶ in his meeting with Nebuchadnezzar?

5 Why was Daniel able to speak prophetically to Nebuchadnezzar? In what was his prophetic gift grounded? What implications does this have for us?

6 In Jerusalem, the Jews had seen their prophets calling their kings to account under God's covenant with them. In Babylon, Daniel's prophecy was a political act, calling the pagan king Nebuchadnezzar to account. What does this say about Daniel's understanding of God and who he is concerned for?

7 What was the essence of Daniel's interpretation of the dream? How would you sum it up in one phrase?

APPLY THIS TO
MY CHURCH

8
A friend was a miner during the British miners' strike of the early 1980s. In this protracted and bitter conflict, which affected every home in the village, the minister did not once refer to any aspect of the strike in either preaching or prayer. The people of this community were left to struggle with almost unendurable realities bereft of any word of wholeness from this official representative of the gospel. The word of life that saved them was ministered to them in the soup kitchens and the homes of the mostly unchurched. No wonder my friend felt betrayed by the church.

Kathy Galloway

Are churches still wary of getting involved in politics like this? Why?

What role do you think the church should play in a situation like the miners' strike that impacts a whole community?

APPLY THIS TO
MY CHURCH

9 Prophecy is not just the act of an individual. How can the church be a prophetic communal voice into our culture? On what current issues do you think your church should have a prophetic voice?

HOW DOES THIS
APPLY TO ME

10 What can we learn from Daniel's example about the way in which we should relate to people when we want to be prophetic?

WORSHIP

From newspapers cut out the current issues that you long for God to speak into, or for the church to have a prophetic voice on. Pray for these areas. Ask God to show you how he might be calling you to speak or act prophetically.

DURING THE WEEK

What view of the future and the end of the world do we get from the media? Watch a film such as *The Day After Tomorrow*, *Minority Report*, *Deep Impact* or *Independence Day* and think about how its worldview contrasts with the Bible's.

FOR FURTHER STUDY

Who has acted as a modern-day prophet in the last century, speaking God's word clearly into our world and calling societies, politicians and individuals to account? Talk about this with other members of your group and discover more about their heroes.

LOOKING TO THE FUTURE

AIM

Aim: To consider what we can learn from the apocalyptic passages in the Bible and how we should approach them

In the first year of Belshazzar king of Babylon, Daniel had a dream, and visions passed through his mind as he was lying on his bed. He wrote down the substance of his dream.

Daniel said: "In my vision at night I looked, and there before me were the four winds of heaven churning up the great sea. Four great beasts, each different from the others, came up out of the sea.

"The first was like a lion, and it had the wings of an eagle. I watched until its wings were torn off and it was lifted from the ground so that it stood on two feet like a man, and the heart of a man was given to it. And there before me was a second beast, which looked like a bear. It was raised up on one of its sides, and it had three ribs in its mouth between its teeth. It was told, 'Get up and eat your fill of flesh!'

"After that, I looked, and there before me was another beast, one that looked like a leopard. And on its back it had four wings like those of a bird. This beast had four heads, and it was given authority to rule. After that, in my vision at night I looked, and there before me was a fourth beast—terrifying and frightening and very powerful. It had large iron teeth; it crushed and devoured its victims and trampled underfoot whatever was left. It was different from all the former beasts, and it had ten horns.

"While I was thinking about the horns, there before me was another horn, a little one, which came up among them; and three of the first horns were uprooted before it. This horn had eyes like the eyes of a man and a mouth that spoke boastfully.

"As I looked,

"thrones were set in place, and the Ancient of Days took his seat. His clothing was as white as snow; the hair of his head was white like wool. His throne was

flaming with fire, and its wheels were all ablaze. A river of fire was flowing, coming out from before him. Thousands upon thousands attended him; ten thousand times ten thousand stood before him. The court was seated, and the books were opened.

"Then I continued to watch because of the boastful words the horn was speaking. I kept looking until the beast was slain and its body destroyed and thrown into the blazing fire. (The other beasts had been stripped of their authority, but were allowed to live for a period of time.)

"In my vision at night I looked, and there before me was one like a son of man, coming with the clouds of heaven. He approached the Ancient of Days and was led into his presence. He was given authority, glory and sovereign power; all peoples, nations and men of every language worshipped him. His dominion is an everlasting dominion that will not pass away, and his kingdom is one that will never be destroyed.

"I, Daniel, was troubled in spirit, and the visions that passed through my mind disturbed me. I approached one of those standing there and asked him the true meaning of all this.

"So he told me and gave me the interpretation of these things: 'The four great beasts are four kingdoms that will rise from the earth. But the saints of the Most High will receive the kingdom and will possess it for ever—yes, for ever and ever.'

"Then I wanted to know the true meaning of the fourth beast, which was different from all the others and most terrifying, with its iron teeth and bronze claws—the beast that crushed and devoured its victims and trampled underfoot whatever was left. I also wanted to know about the ten horns on its head and about the other horn that came up, before which three of them fell—the horn that looked more imposing than the others and that had eyes and a mouth that spoke boastfully. As I watched, this horn was waging war against the saints and defeating them, until the Ancient of Days came and pronounced judgment in favour of the saints of the Most High, and the time came when they possessed the kingdom.

"He gave me this explanation: 'The fourth beast is a fourth kingdom that will appear on earth. It will be different from all the other kingdoms and will devour the whole earth, trampling it down and crushing it. The ten horns are ten kings who will come from this kingdom. After them another king will arise, different from the earlier ones; he will subdue three kings. He will speak against the

Most High and oppress his saints and try to change the set times and the laws. The saints will be handed over to him for a time, times and half a time.

"'But the court will sit, and his power will be taken away and completely destroyed for ever. Then the sovereignty, power and greatness of the kingdoms under the whole heaven will be handed over to the saints, the people of the Most High. His kingdom will be an everlasting kingdom, and all rulers will worship and obey him.'

"This is the end of the matter. I, Daniel, was deeply troubled by my thoughts, and my face turned pale, but I kept the matter to myself."

Daniel 7

TO SET THE SCENE
Discuss the films that people watched during the week. What view of the end of the world do they give?

Read the passage together
1 What's your response to this passage? What questions do you have?

2 What similarities are there between Daniel's vision and Nebuchadnezzar's dream?

HOW DOES THIS ... APPLY TO ME?

3 How should we interpret biblical passages like this? What extremes can we fall into when trying to understand apocalyptic writings?

What is the central message of Daniel's vision?

WHAT DOES ... THE BIBLE SAY?

4 As we've seen, not all prophecy is predictive – talking about the future – but some is. Look at these passages from the New Testament. What value did the early church give the predictive nature of prophecy?

▶ Acts 2:14–36
Peter preaches on the day of Pentecost

- ▶ Acts 13:32–43
  Paul preaches in Pisidian Antioch
- ▶ Acts 8:26–35
  Philip is directed to talk to the Ethiopian eunuch
- ▶ 2 Peter 3:1–18
  Peter talks about the future day of the Lord
- ▶ Revelation 1:1–3, 4:1–11
  John's vision in the book of Revelation.

What implications does this have for us?

5 Apocalyptic writing, like this passage, is rich in metaphor – throwing light on different concepts by relating them to what we know, for example by describing God as a Rock. What other metaphors for God are used in the Bible? How do they help us to understand God better? Which have been particularly meaningful to you?

6 Metaphors are never exact parallels; they have limitations. Although God is described as a shepherd, a father, a warrior, he is not exactly like or limited to being a shepherd or a father or a warrior. What are the limitations of the metaphors for God that you have just discussed?

ENGAGING WITH

THE WORLD

7 How would you explain to someone who is not a Christian how they should understand this passage from Daniel?

WORSHIP

The psalms are the most obviously poetic part of the Bible. Find your favourite verses in the psalms – they could be words of praise, or lament, or declarations of faith – whatever seems appropriate to the theme of this week. Read these out as you pray together.

DURING THE WEEK

Look out for people talking about the future in conversations, on the news, in news-papers and on TV. What are they expecting to happen? Is it positive or negative? Who is regarded as having authority to speak about the future? What part does God play in society's contemplation of the future?

FOR FURTHER STUDY

Look at the way that Jesus communicated with people in Matthew's gospel, noting any differences in the way he spoke to his disciples (for example Mt. 5–7), the Pharisees (Mt. 21:23 – 22:14) and the crowds of people (Mt. 13:1–10, 24–35). How differently might the world receive the message of the church if it was delivered in the questioning, inviting style of Jesus himself?

STANDING UNDER PRESSURE

AIM

Aim: to consider the effect that pressure has on our faith, and how we can stand firm under it

King Nebuchadnezzar made an image of gold, ninety feet high and nine feet wide, and set it up on the plain of Dura in the province of Babylon. He then summoned the satraps, prefects, governors, advisers, treasurers, judges, magistrates and all the other provincial officials to come to the dedication of the image he had set up. So the satraps, prefects, governors, advisers, treasurers, judges, magistrates and all the other provincial officials assembled for the dedication of the image that King Nebuchadnezzar had set up, and they stood before it.

Then the herald loudly proclaimed, "This is what you are commanded to do, O peoples, nations and men of every language: As soon as you hear the sound of the horn, flute, zither, lyre, harp, pipes and all kinds of music, you must fall down and worship the image of gold that King Nebuchadnezzar has set up. Whoever does not fall down and worship will immediately be thrown into a blazing furnace." Therefore, as soon as they heard the sound of the horn, flute, zither, lyre, harp and all kinds of music, all the peoples, nations and men of every language fell down and worshipped the image of gold that King Nebuchadnezzar had set up.

At this time some astrologers came forward and denounced the Jews. They said to King Nebuchadnezzar, "O king, live forever! You have issued a decree, O king, that everyone who hears the sound of the horn, flute, zither, lyre, harp, pipes and all kinds of music must fall down and worship the image of gold, and that whoever does not fall down and worship will be thrown into a blazing furnace. But there are some Jews whom you have set over the affairs of the province of Babylon—Shadrach, Meshach and Abednego—who pay no attention to you, O king. They neither serve your gods nor worship the image of gold you have set up."

Furious with rage, Nebuchadnezzar summoned Shadrach, Meshach and Abednego. So these men were brought before the king, and Nebuchadnezzar said to them, "Is it true, Shadrach, Meshach and Abednego, that you do not serve my gods or worship the image of gold I have set up? Now when you hear the sound of the horn, flute, zither, lyre, harp, pipes and all kinds of music, if you are ready to fall down and worship the image I made, very good. But if you do not worship it, you will be thrown immediately into a blazing furnace. Then what god will be able to rescue you from my hand?"

Shadrach, Meshach and Abednego replied to the king, "O Nebuchadnezzar, we do not need to defend ourselves before you in this matter. If we are thrown into the blazing furnace, the God we serve is able to save us from it, and he will rescue us from your hand, O king. But even if he does not, we want you to know, O king, that we will not serve your gods or worship the image of gold you have set up."

Then Nebuchadnezzar was furious with Shadrach, Meshach and Abednego, and his attitude towards them changed. He ordered the furnace to be heated seven times hotter than usual and commanded some of the strongest soldiers in his army to tie up Shadrach, Meshach and Abednego and throw them into the blazing furnace. So these men, wearing their robes, trousers, turbans and other clothes, were bound and thrown into the blazing furnace. The king's command was so urgent and the furnace so hot that the flames of the fire killed the soldiers who took up Shadrach, Meshach and Abednego, and these three men, firmly tied, fell into the blazing furnace.

Then King Nebuchadnezzar leaped to his feet in amazement and asked his advisers, "Weren't there three men that we tied up and threw into the fire?"

They replied, "Certainly, O king."

He said, "Look! I see four men walking around in the fire, unbound and unharmed, and the fourth looks like a son of the gods."

Nebuchadnezzar then approached the opening of the blazing furnace and shouted, "Shadrach, Meshach and Abednego, servants of the Most High God, come out! Come here!"

So Shadrach, Meshach and Abednego came out of the fire, and the satraps, prefects, governors and royal advisers crowded around them. They saw that the fire had not harmed their bodies, nor was a hair of their heads singed; their robes were not scorched, and there was no smell of fire on them.

Then Nebuchadnezzar said, "Praise be to the God of Shadrach, Meshach and Abednego, who has sent his angel and rescued his servants! They trusted in him and defied the king's command and were willing to give up their lives rather than serve or worship any god except their own God. Therefore I decree that the people of any nation or language who say anything against the God of Shadrach, Meshach and Abednego be cut into pieces and their houses be turned into piles of rubble, for no other god can save in this way."

Then the king promoted Shadrach, Meshach and Abednego in the province of Babylon.

Daniel 3

TO SET THE SCENE

Take a piece of play dough and form it into a shape that represents how your week has been. Then tell the rest of the group about it.

Read the passage together.

HOW DOES THIS APPLY TO ME

1 The faith of the Jewish exiles is under pressure yet again. Compared to Daniel and his friends, how much pressure has your faith come under and why?

2 Living in a foreign culture, Shadrach, Meshach and Abednego have had to live very different lifestyles to the ones that they had in Jerusalem. In this story, they have a big confrontation with the culture in which they live. What issue is at stake? Which of God's commandments is Nebuchadnezzar challenging?

AN ABOMINATION TO GOD

Idolatry is described in the Bible as the gravest sin, as spiritual adultery. It violates the heart of the covenant and the first and second commandments. And yet throughout the story of Israel the people repeatedly turn to idol worship. The idol is nothing but a man-made token, a futile, powerless gesture. And yet there remains somehow a demonic spiritual force behind it, so that the practice of idolatry brings man into contact with forces of evil. Idolatry is an abomination to God.

An idol can be anything that comes before God in our lives. Just as Israel had to come out from slavery in Egypt to worship God in the desert, in order to serve God in worship, one must be free from service to other things.

Look up Isaiah 44:9–20, 1 Corinthians 8:4, 10:19–20, Deuteronomy 31:16–19

3 What in our culture demands our allegiance? What are the 'god-substitutes' that people around us worship? What kind of expressions of worship are they paid?

4 Why do you think Shadrach, Meshach and Abednego made such a courageous stand over this issue?

In verses 17,18 they effectively say, 'God will rescue us, but even if he doesn't he is still God.' Does this show faith or doubt?

HOW DOES THIS

APPLY TO ME

5 Think about how you pray when you are under pressure.

Philip Yancey says,
In my travel overseas I have noticed a striking difference in the wording of prayers. Christians in affluent countries tend to pray, 'Lord take this trial away from us!' I have heard

*prisoners, persecuted Christians, and some who
live in very poor countries pray instead, 'Lord
give us the strength to bear this trial.'*

Which does God do for Shadrach, Meshach and
Abednego? How can we move towards the second
approach – and should we? Look at James 1:2–4.

HOW DOES THIS

APPLY TO ME

6 Stories from the persecuted church tell
us that even in the worst of circumstances
joy is found. Richard Wurmbrand, who suf-
fered years of imprisonment, torture and
inhumanity because of his faith, writes, 'I suffer in the
West more than I did in Communist lands. My suffering consists first of all in longing for the unspeakable
beauties of the underground Church, the church that
fulfils the old Latin saying *nudis nudum Christi sequi*
(naked, follow the naked Christ). ... I have found truly
joyful Christians only in the Bible, in the underground
church and in prison.'

What is your response to his words? Have you seen
or experienced adversity or suffering that has led to
the joy that Richard is talking about?

7 If the sufferings of the body of Christ call us to
'stand as one' and to weep with those who weep,
what might the implications be for our involvement
with the suffering church, in our prayers and the
worship lives of our churches?

ENGAGING WITH

THE WORLD

8 In our own culture and context, is direct
opposition to the Christian faith likely to
increase or decrease in the years ahead?
What effect will that have on your churches
and our own practice of faith? What will need to
change?

9 What does God do for Shadrach, Meshach and
Abednego as a result of their obedience to him?

10 How does their action affect Nebuchadnezzar?

WORSHIP

Read some stories of Christians who are being persecuted for their faith. Use the story that you have just read to inspire your prayers for them. Leave your finger-prints on their pictures to show that you have stood alongside them and prayed for them.

DURING THE WEEK

Look out for situations in the news that will put Christians around the world under pressure in different ways. Pray for Christians who will be affected, that God will strengthen them through their trial and that their suffering will bear fruit.

FOR FURTHER STUDY

Read the stories of people who have been persecuted for their faith. Try one of these books, or ask others in your group to recommend a book that they have read.

Imprisoned in Iran by Dan Baumann (YWAM publishing, 2000)
Dan's own account of his arrest and imprisonment in Tehran, when he was falsely accused of espionage while travelling with YWAM.

The Tears of My Soul by Sokreaksa S. Himm (Oxford: Monarch, 2003)
A powerful story of the triumph of forgiveness over hatred. Sokreaksa was the only member of his family to escape from Cambodia's killing fields.

Tortured for Christ by Richard Wurmbrand (London: Hodder & Stoughton, 2004)
A personal account of imprisonment and torture in Romania in the very worst moments of the Communist era.

FIGHTING SEDUCTION

Aim: to consider when we need to make a stand in our Christian lives to explore the importance of a life of regular prayer

It pleased Darius to appoint 120 satraps to rule throughout the kingdom, with three administrators over them, one of whom was Daniel. The satraps were made accountable to them so that the king might not suffer loss. Now Daniel so distinguished himself among the administrators and the satraps by his exceptional qualities that the king planned to set him over the whole kingdom. At this, the administrators and the satraps tried to find grounds for charges against Daniel in his conduct of government affairs, but they were unable to do so. They could find no corruption in him, because he was trustworthy and neither corrupt nor negligent. Finally these men said, "We will never find any basis for charges against this man Daniel unless it has something to do with the law of his God."

So the administrators and the satraps went as a group to the king and said: "O King Darius, live forever! The royal administrators, prefects, satraps, advisers and governors have all agreed that the king should issue an edict and enforce the decree that anyone who prays to any god or man during the next thirty days, except to you, O king, shall be thrown into the lions' den. Now, O king, issue the decree and put it in writing so that it cannot be altered—in accordance with the laws of the Medes and Persians, which cannot be repealed." So King Darius put the decree in writing.

Now when Daniel learned that the decree had been published, he went home to his upstairs room where the windows opened toward Jerusalem. Three times a day he got down on his knees and prayed, giving thanks to his God, just as he had done before. Then these men went as a group and found Daniel pray-ing and asking God for help. So they went to the king and spoke to him about his royal decree: "Did you not publish a decree that during the next thirty days anyone who prays to any god or man except to you, O king, would be thrown into the lions' den?"

The king answered, "The decree stands—in accordance with the laws of the Medes and Persians, which cannot be repealed."

Then they said to the king, "Daniel, who is one of the exiles from Judah, pays no attention to you, O king, or to the decree you put in writing. He still prays three times a day." When the king heard this, he was greatly distressed; he was determined to rescue Daniel and made every effort until sundown to save him.

Then the men went as a group to the king and said to him, "Remember, O king, that according to the law of the Medes and Persians no decree or edict that the king issues can be changed."

So the king gave the order, and they brought Daniel and threw him into the lions' den. The king said to Daniel, "May your God, whom you serve continually, rescue you!"

A stone was brought and placed over the mouth of the den, and the king sealed it with his own signet ring and with the rings of his nobles, so that Daniel's situation might not be changed. Then the king returned to his palace and spent the night without eating and without any entertainment being brought to him. And he could not sleep.

At the first light of dawn, the king got up and hurried to the lions' den. When he came near the den, he called to Daniel in an anguished voice, "Daniel, servant of the living God, has your God, whom you serve continually, been able to rescue you from the lions?"

Daniel answered, "O king, live forever! My God sent his angel, and he shut the mouths of the lions. They have not hurt me, because I was found innocent in his sight. Nor have I ever done any wrong before you, O king."

The king was overjoyed and gave orders to lift Daniel out of the den. And when Daniel was lifted from the den, no wound was found on him, because he had trusted in his God.

At the king's command, the men who had falsely accused Daniel were brought in and thrown into the lions' den, along with their wives and children. And before they reached the floor of the den, the lions overpowered them and crushed all their bones.

Then King Darius wrote to all the peoples, nations and men of every language throughout the land:

"May you prosper greatly!

"I issue a decree that in every part of my kingdom people must fear and reverence the God of Daniel.

"For he is the living God and he endures for ever; his kingdom will not be destroyed, his dominion will never end. He rescues and he saves; he performs signs and wonders in the heavens and on the earth. He has rescued Daniel from the power of the lions."

So Daniel prospered during the reign of Darius and the reign of Cyrus the Persian.

Daniel 6

TO SET THE SCENE

Talk about the regular routines that you follow each day or each week. How predictable are you? How long have those routines been going? What makes you stick to them?

Read the passage together.

1 The stories of the fiery furnace and the den of lions have certain similarities. What parallels can you see in these two stories? What is the subtle difference?

2 Daniel's enemies knew just how to trap him (v5) and exactly when to find him praying (v11). What does this tell us about Daniel's faith?

ENGAGING WITH

THE WORLD

3 In our society we aren't confronted with golden idols; nor are we commanded not to pray. What things in our lives and in our society make it difficult for us to pray?

APPLY THIS TO

MY CHURCH

4 In what ways are Christians and churches most likely to be seduced by the culture's dominant ideas?

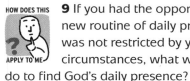

HOW DOES THIS **5** Daniel and his friends lived lives of quiet nonconformity. They didn't see the reform of Babylonian culture as their priority, but **APPLY TO ME** they were prepared to make a public stand when it was really important. How do you decide when you need to make a public stand – at home, at work, in your study, at church, among your friends?

HOW DOES THIS **6** Daniel got into trouble because he prayed. Talk honestly about the place of prayer in your life. Do you make a regular **APPLY TO ME** time for prayer? When does prayer most easily flow? When is prayer most difficult? What has enriched your prayer life?

7 Prayer was a crucial part of Daniel's life – not just something that he turned to in difficult times. How can you weave prayer into the fabric of your daily life?

Have times of regular, ordinary prayer helped you when you have faced the extraordinary?

8 Who else prays in this story (v16)? What is striking about this prayer and the person who prays it?

HOW DOES THIS **9** If you had the opportunity to carve out a new routine of daily prayer and your time was not restricted by your home and work **APPLY TO ME** circumstances, what would you choose to do to find God's daily presence?

Is there any way you can incorporate any of that ideal into your normal life?

WORSHIP

*There is an awakening among many believers today who are no longer satis-
fied with the hustle and bustle generally known as the Christian life. Call it the
deeper life, the contemplative life, or whatever you will. By any name this quality of Christian life is conceived in divine intimacy and born in quiet moments
spent between two lovers. Many Christians who are dissatisfied with the empti-
ness of the noise are hearing his gentle call to something deeper, richer.*

Steve McVey

Spend some time in silent prayer; enjoy resting in God's presence.

DURING THE WEEK

Make space for prayer. Even if it is ten minutes per day, even if you say nothing but
just sit in God's presence, even if you have to get up earlier to do it – make some
space each day to be with God.

FOR FURTHER STUDY

Study Daniel's prayers in chapter 2 and chapter 9. What does the way that Daniel
prayed tell you about him and his faith? What does it tell you about God? What can
you learn from these prayers?

UNDERSTANDING POWER

AIM

Aim: to think through a right attitude to power

King Nebuchadnezzar,

To the peoples, nations and men of every language, who live in all the world:

May you prosper greatly!

It is my pleasure to tell you about the miraculous signs and wonders that the Most High God has performed for me.

How great are his signs, how mighty his wonders! His kingdom is an eternal kingdom; his dominion endures from generation to generation.

I, Nebuchadnezzar, was at home in my palace, contented and prosperous. I had a dream that made me afraid. As I was lying in my bed, the images and visions that passed through my mind terrified me. So I commanded that all the wise men of Babylon be brought before me to interpret the dream for me. When the magicians, enchanters, astrologers and diviners came, I told them the dream, but they could not interpret it for me. Finally, Daniel came into my presence and I told him the dream. (He is called Belteshazzar, after the name of my god, and the spirit of the holy gods is in him.)

I said, "Belteshazzar, chief of the magicians, I know that the spirit of the holy gods is in you, and no mystery is too difficult for you. Here is my dream; interpret it for me. These are the visions I saw while lying in my bed: I looked, and there before me stood a tree in the middle of the land. Its height was enormous. The tree grew large and strong and its top touched the sky; it was visible to the ends of the earth. Its leaves were beautiful, its fruit abundant, and on it was food for all. Under it the beasts of the field found shelter, and the birds of the air lived in its branches; from it every creature was fed.

"In the visions I saw while lying in my bed, I looked, and there before me was a messenger, a holy one, coming down from heaven. He called in a loud voice: 'Cut down the tree and trim off its branches; strip off its leaves and scatter its

fruit. Let the animals flee from under it and the birds from its branches. But let the stump and its roots, bound with iron and bronze, remain in the ground, in the grass of the field.

"'Let him be drenched with the dew of heaven, and let him live with the animals among the plants of the earth. Let his mind be changed from that of a man and let him be given the mind of an animal, till seven times pass by for him.

"'The decision is announced by messengers, the holy ones declare the verdict, so that the living may know that the Most High is sovereign over the kingdoms of men and gives them to anyone he wishes and sets over them the lowliest of men.'

"This is the dream that I, King Nebuchadnezzar, had. Now, Belteshazzar, tell me what it means, for none of the wise men in my kingdom can interpret it for me. But you can, because the spirit of the holy gods is in you."

Then Daniel (also called Belteshazzar) was greatly perplexed for a time, and his thoughts terrified him. So the king said, "Belteshazzar, do not let the dream or its meaning alarm you."

Belteshazzar answered, "My lord, if only the dream applied to your enemies and its meaning to your adversaries! The tree you saw, which grew large and strong, with its top touching the sky, visible to the whole earth, with beautiful leaves and abundant fruit, providing food for all, giving shelter to the beasts of the field, and having nesting places in its branches for the birds of the air—you, O king, are that tree! You have become great and strong; your greatness has grown until it reaches the sky, and your dominion extends to distant parts of the earth.

"You, O king, saw a messenger, a holy one, coming down from heaven and saying, 'Cut down the tree and destroy it, but leave the stump, bound with iron and bronze, in the grass of the field, while its roots remain in the ground. Let him be drenched with the dew of heaven; let him live like the wild animals, until seven times pass by for him.'

"This is the interpretation, O king, and this is the decree the Most High has issued against my lord the king: You will be driven away from people and will live with the wild animals; you will eat grass like cattle and be drenched with the dew of heaven. Seven times will pass by for you until you acknowledge that the Most High is sovereign over the kingdoms of men and gives them to anyone he wishes. The command to leave the stump of the tree with its roots means *that your kingdom will be restored to you when you acknowledge that Heaven rules. Therefore, O king, be pleased to accept my advice: Renounce your sins by doing what is right, and your wickedness by being kind to the oppressed. It may be that then your prosperity will continue.*

All this happened to King Nebuchadnezzar. Twelve months later, as the king was walking on the roof of the royal palace of Babylon, he said, "Is not this the great Babylon I have built as the royal residence, by my mighty power and for the glory of my majesty?"

The words were still on his lips when a voice came from heaven, "This is what is decreed for you, King Nebuchadnezzar: Your royal authority has been taken from you. You will be driven away from people and will live with the wild animals; you will eat grass like cattle. Seven times will pass by for you until you acknowledge that the Most High is sovereign over the kingdoms of men and gives them to anyone he wishes."

Immediately what had been said about Nebuchadnezzar was fulfilled. He was driven away from people and ate grass like cattle. His body was drenched with the dew of heaven until his hair grew like the feathers of an eagle and his nails like the claws of a bird.

At the end of that time, I, Nebuchadnezzar, raised my eyes towards heaven, and my sanity was restored. Then I praised the Most High; I honoured and glorified him who lives for ever.

His dominion is an eternal dominion; his kingdom endures from generation to generation.

All the peoples of the earth are regarded as nothing. He does as he pleases with the powers of heaven and the peoples of the earth. No-one can hold back his hand or say to him: "What have you done?"

At the same time that my sanity was restored, my honour and splendour were returned to me for the glory of my kingdom. My advisers and nobles sought me out, and I was restored to my throne and became even greater than before. Now I, Nebuchadnezzar, praise and exalt and glorify the King of heaven, because everything he does is right and all his ways are just. And those who walk in pride he is able to humble.

Daniel 4

TO SET THE SCENE

Who do you think are the most powerful people in the world? Why? What power do they have? Who are the most powerful people in this country? In your life? What power do you have?

Read the passage together

1 In what ways has Nebuchadnezzar encountered God in the last few chapters? Why do you think those encounters have not had a lasting effect on him?

2 How much power does Nebuchadnezzar have? Think back over what we have seen him do so far. How does Daniel talk about Nebuchadnezzar's power?

What power does Daniel have?

3 What does this passage show about God's power?

4 Read what Jesus said about power when he stood before Pilate in John 19:1–11. Is that true of all earthly power today? Can we say of Saddam Hussein, George Bush, Tony Blair, that they had or have power only because God has given it to them? What questions does that raise for you?

WHAT DOES
SEARCH
THE BIBLE SAY?

5 Read these verses from the New Testament. What do they have to say about God's power and about us?

Acts 1:8	1 John 4:4
Matthew 17:20	1 Corinthians 2:1–5

WHAT DOES
SEARCH
THE BIBLE SAY?

6 How did Jesus use his power when he was here on earth?

John 13:1–5	Matthew 20:20–28
Matthew 10:1–10	Matthew 21:12–17
Matthew 26:47–56	

APPLY THIS TO MY CHURCH

7 How good has the church been in following Jesus' example in terms of its attitude to power? Can you think of examples of both abuses of the church's power, and good uses of its power?

8 If we treated power in the same way that Jesus did, what impact would that have on the way we do mission?

APPLY THIS TO MY CHURCH

9 If we were committed to working with the understanding of power that seeks to serve rather than dominate, what might change about the way we function as a church?

WORSHIP

What power do you have in different areas of your life? How do you use that power? Put symbols of your power in the centre of the group. Pray that God will help you to use your power to serve rather than to dominate. Take your symbols of power back with care.

DURING THE WEEK

Next week we'll look at Daniel's faithfulness to God over his lifetime. Arrange to meet with an older Christian that you know who has been faithful to God throughout their life. If it's not possible to meet, you could talk on the phone. What trials have they been through? What joys have they experienced? What has kept them going? How would they sum up their relationship with God? What advice would they give you to help you keep your faith for the long haul?

FOR FURTHER STUDY

Read Paul's words about Jesus' approach to power in Philippians 2:5–11. What other biblical examples are there of God using the powerless to confront and challenge those in power? Have a look at Moses, Gideon and David when he confronted Goliath for a start.

FINISHING WELL

Aim: to explore how we can remain faithful servants of God throughout our lives

King Belshazzar gave a great banquet for a thousand of his nobles and drank wine with them. While Belshazzar was drinking his wine, he gave orders to bring in the gold and silver goblets that Nebuchadnezzar his father had taken from the temple in Jerusalem, so that the king and his nobles, his wives and his concubines might drink from them. So they brought in the gold goblets that had been taken from the temple of God in Jerusalem, and the king and his nobles, his wives and his concubines drank from them. As they drank the wine, they praised the gods of gold and silver, of bronze, iron, wood and stone.

Suddenly the fingers of a human hand appeared and wrote on the plaster of the wall, near the lampstand in the royal palace. The king watched the hand as it wrote. His face turned pale and he was so frightened that his knees knocked together and his legs gave way.

The king called out for the enchanters, astrologers and diviners to be brought and said to these wise men of Babylon, "Whoever reads this writing and tells me what it means will be clothed in purple and have a gold chain placed around his neck, and he will be made the third highest ruler in the kingdom."

Then all the king's wise men came in, but they could not read the writing or tell the king what it meant. So King Belshazzar became even more terrified and his face grew more pale. His nobles were baffled.

The queen, hearing the voices of the king and his nobles, came into the banquet hall. "O king, live for ever!" she said. "Don't be alarmed! Don't look so pale! There is a man in your kingdom who has the spirit of the holy gods in him. In the time of your father he was found to have insight and intelligence and wisdom like that of the gods. King Nebuchadnezzar your father—your father the king, I say—appointed him chief of the magicians, enchanters, astrologers and diviners. This man Daniel, whom the king called Belteshazzar, was found to have a keen mind and knowledge and understanding, and also the ability to interpret dreams, explain riddles and solve difficult problems. Call for Daniel, and he will tell you what the writing means."

So Daniel was brought before the king, and the king said to him, "Are you Daniel, one of the exiles my father the king brought from Judah? I have heard that the spirit of the gods is in you and that you have insight, intelligence and outstanding wisdom. The wise men and enchanters were brought before me to read this writing and tell me what it means, but they could not explain it. Now I have heard that you are able to give interpretations and to solve difficult problems. If you can read this writing and tell me what it means, you will be clothed in purple and have a gold chain placed around your neck, and you will be made the third highest ruler in the kingdom."

Then Daniel answered the king, "You may keep your gifts for yourself and give your rewards to someone else. Nevertheless, I will read the writing for the king and tell him what it means.

"O king, the Most High God gave your father Nebuchadnezzar sovereignty and greatness and glory and splendour. Because of the high position he gave him, all the peoples and nations and men of every language dreaded and feared him. Those the king wanted to put to death, he put to death; those he wanted to spare, he spared; those he wanted to promote, he promoted; and those he wanted to humble, he humbled. But when his heart became arrogant and hardened with pride, he was deposed from his royal throne and stripped of his glory. He was driven away from people and given the mind of an animal; he lived with the wild donkeys and ate grass like cattle; and his body was drenched with the dew of heaven, until he acknowledged that the Most High God is sovereign over the kingdoms of men and sets over them anyone he wishes.

"But you his son, O Belshazzar, have not humbled yourself, though you knew all this. Instead, you have set yourself up against the Lord of heaven. You had the goblets from his temple brought to you, and you and your nobles, your wives and your concubines drank wine from them. You praised the gods of silver and gold, of bronze, iron, wood and stone, which cannot see or hear or understand. But you did not honour the God who holds in his hand your life and all your ways. Therefore he sent the hand that wrote the inscription.

"This is the inscription that was written:

MENE, MENE, TEKEL, PARSIN

"This is what these words mean:

Mene: God has numbered the days of your reign and brought it to an end.
Tekel: You have been weighed on the scales and found wanting.
Peres: Your kingdom is divided and given to the Medes and Persians."

Then at Belshazzar's command, Daniel was clothed in purple, a gold chain was placed around his neck, and he was proclaimed the third highest ruler in the kingdom.

That very night Belshazzar, king of the Babylonians, was slain, and Darius the Mede took over the kingdom, at the age of sixty-two.

Daniel 5

TO SET THE SCENE
Talk about the older Christians that you met or talked to in the week. What did you learn from them?

Read the passage together.
1 The events of this chapter happened about sixty years after chapter 4, but there are some parallels between the two stories. What similarities and what differences can you see?

2 What is the significance of Belshazzar and his cronies drinking from the goblets taken from the Jewish temple?

3 Belshazzar's appearance in the book of Daniel is brief. What can you learn from him?

4 In these chapters we have read about some dramatic incidents in Daniel's life. How do you think he behaved in the non-dramatic moments?

HOW DOES THIS
APPLY TO ME

5 How long have you been a Christian? Have you survived or thrived? What has helped you to persevere?

6 Have you ever been in danger of losing your faith? What do you think is the biggest threat to your faith?

7 What part can Christians play in helping each other to persevere? How have other Christians helped you in your faith so far? What else could you do for each other?

8 Read how the book of Daniel ends in Daniel 12:13. *The Message* puts it like this:

> *And you? Go about your business without fretting or worrying. Relax. When it's all over, you will be on your feet to receive your reward.*

When the book of Daniel ends, he is still in exile. How do you think the experience has changed him? What has he learned about God?

9 What will you take away from this series of studies? Share the moments that have had the biggest impact on you. Talk about any questions you still have.

WORSHIP

Bring those thoughts and experiences to God in prayer, thanking him for what he has shown you and asking him to help you through the questions you still have.

Sing a song of praise and worship to God, as an affirmation that you will sing the Lord's song in the middle of a culture that does not acknowledge him.

LEADERS' GUIDE

TO HELP YOU LEAD

You may have led a housegroup many times before or this may be your first time. Here is some advice on how to lead these studies:

▶ As a group leader, you don't have to be an expert or a lecturer. You are there to facilitate the learning of the group members – helping them to discover for themselves the wisdom in God's word. You should not be doing most of the talking or dishing out the answers, whatever the group expects from you!

▶ You do need to be aware of the group's dynamics, however. People can be quite quick to label themselves and each other in a group situation. One person might be seen as the expert, another the moaner who always has something to complain about. One person may be labelled as quiet and not be expected to contribute; another person may always jump in with something to say. Be aware of the different type of individuals in the group, but don't allow the labels to stick. You may need to encourage those who find it hard to get a word in, and quieten down those who always have something to say. Talk to members between sessions to find out how they feel about the group.

▶ The sessions are planned to try and engage every member in actively learning. Of course you cannot force anyone to take part if they don't want to, but it won't be too easy to be a spectator. Activities that ask everyone to write down a word, or to talk in twos and then report back to the group, are there for a reason. They give everyone space to think and form their opinion, even if not everyone voices it out loud.

▶ Do adapt the sessions for your group as you feel is appropriate. Some groups may know each other very well and be prepared to talk at a deep level. New groups may take a bit of time to get to know each other before making themselves vulnerable, but encourage members to share their lives with each other.

▶ Encourage a number of replies to each question. The study is not about finding a single right answer, but about sharing experiences and thoughts in order to find out how to apply the Bible to people's lives. When brainstorming, don't be too quick to evaluate the contributions. Write everything down and then have a look to see which suggestions are worth keeping.

▶ Similarly encourage everyone to ask questions, to voice doubts and to discuss difficulties. Some parts of the Bible are difficult to understand. Sometimes the Christian faith throws up paradoxes. Painful things happen to us that make it difficult to see what God is doing. A housegroup should be a safe place to express all of this. If discussion doesn't resolve the issue, send everyone away to pray about it, in between sessions, and ask your minister for advice!

- Give yourself time in the week to read through the Bible passage and the questions. Read the Leaders' notes for the session, as different ways of presenting the questions are sometimes suggested. However, during the session, don't be too quick to come in with the answer – sometimes we need space to think.
- Delegate as much as you like! The easiest activities to delegate are reading the text, and the worship suggestions, but there are other ways to involve group members. Giving people responsibility can help them own the session much more.
- Pray for group members by name, that God would meet with them during the week. Pray for the group session, for a constructive and helpful time. Ask the Lord to equip you as you lead the group.

THE STRUCTURE OF EACH SESSION

Although specific feedback activities are not always given, we do suggest that at the start of each session you find out what people remember from the previous session, or if they have been able to act during the week on what was discussed last time.

To set the scene: an activity or a question to get everyone thinking about the subject to be studied.

Bible reading: it's important actually to read the passage you are studying during the session. Ask someone to prepare this in advance or go round the group reading a verse or two each. Don't assume everyone will be happy to read out loud.

Questions and activities: adapt these as appropriate to your group. Some groups may enjoy a more activity-based approach; some may prefer just to discuss the questions. Try out some new things!

Worship: suggestions for creative worship and prayer are included, which give everyone an opportunity to respond to God, largely individually. Use these alongside singing or other group expressions of worship. Add in a prayer time with opportunities to pray for group members and their families and friends. If you feel the suggestion in the book wouldn't work with your group, then feel free to do something different.

During the week: this gives a specific task to do during the week, helping people to continue to think about or apply what they have learned.

For further study: suggestions are given for those people who want to study the themes further. These could be included in the housegroup if you feel it is appropriate and if there is time.

WHAT YOU NEED

A list of materials that are needed is printed at the start of each session in the Leaders' guide. In addition you will need:

Bibles: a Bible passage for each study is printed in the book so that all the members can work from the same version. You will also need other Bibles available, or to ask everyone to bring their own, so that the other passages referred to can be looked up.

Paper and pens: for people who need more space than is in the book or for specific activities.

Flip chart: it is helpful to write down people's comments during a brainstorming session, so that none of the suggestions is lost. There may not be space for a proper flip chart in the average lounge, and having one may make it feel too much like a business meeting or lecture. Try getting someone to write on a big sheet of paper on the floor or coffee table, and then stick this up on the wall with blu-tack.

GROUND RULES

How do people know what is expected of them in a housegroup situation? Is it ever discussed, or do we just pick up cues from each other? You may find it helpful to discuss some ground rules for the housegroup at the start of this course, even if your group has been going a long time. This also gives you an opportunity to talk about how you, as the leader, see the group. Ask everyone to think about what they want to get out of the course. How do they want the group to work? What values do they want to be part of the group's experience; honesty, respect, confidentiality? How do they want their contributions to be treated? You could ask everyone to write down three ground rules on slips of paper and put them in a bowl. Pass the bowl round the group. Each person takes out a rule and reads it, and someone collates a list. Discuss the ground rules that have been suggested and come up with a top five. This method enables everyone to contribute fairly anonymously. Alternatively, if your group are all quite vocal, have a straight discussion about it!

ICONS

The aim of the session

Engaging with the world

Investigate what else the Bible says

How does this apply to me?

What about my church?

NB not all questions in each session are covered, some are self-explanatory

SESSION 1

YOU WILL NEED

▶ A CD of instrumental worship music and a CD player.

TO SET THE SCENE

The HSBC adverts show interesting cultural differences from around the world. Encourage people to share their feelings over living in a different culture, not just what they did. This will help them to empathise in some small way with the Israelites being taken into exile.

2 God had warned the Israelites time and again that if they didn't walk in his ways, stop worshipping other gods and worship him only then they would be taken into exile. They had been given the chance to repent and turn back to him.

3 God had promised that Israel would have a land of its own. He had promised that they would have descendants and therefore a future. And he had promised that he would be their God and they would be his people – a special relationship. But God himself sent the people into exile. It must have been devastating and shaken the foundations of their faith. Had God lost his power? Did his promises mean nothing? Were the Babylonian gods stronger after all?

4 Not only was this a political victory for the Babylonians, it was also a spiritual victory. The worship of God was being taken over by the worship of the Babylonian gods.

5 They lost their freedom; although they were living in luxurious surroundings and were well looked after, they were effectively prisoners. They lost the ability to worship freely in the way that they chose, among their own community. They lost their names, and more importantly their sense of identity as part of the chosen people of God.

6 Daniel was named after Nebuchadnezzar's god – not exactly a neutral name. Perhaps this is an example of Daniel's wisdom in knowing which battles to fight. Perhaps he had little choice in accepting his name, but he realised that he could exercise influence over what he ate. The parallel for us to take action where we can.

7 Encourage people to dream dreams! Invite people to discuss this question in twos for a few minutes and then feedback their ideas to the rest of the group. Ask for one comment from each pair in turn, going round the group a couple of times until all the ideas have been heard. This will enable everyone to engage with the question rather than discussion being led by a few.

WORSHIP

Allow some space for people to think of friends and situations that need prayer. You could play some instrumental worship music for a few minutes as people think. Read Psalm 13 over the music and invite people to add their prayers, verbally or in silence. Close with a prayer committing this series to God and asking that you will all be open to learning from him.

FOR NEXT WEEK

You may find it useful to have a couple of songs to play snippets of to people as an example of what they need to look out for. For example, you could play 'I want more part one' by Faithless from their album *No Roots* (Arista). It talks about someone who continually whines that they want more, in spite of all the possessions they have. People don't have to choose contemporary pop songs. There are probably examples from whatever genre of music they like!

SESSION 2

YOU WILL NEED

▸ Copies of today's newspapers, a large sheet of paper, scissors and glue sticks.

▸ Some gold and silver paints, paintbrushes.

TO SET THE SCENE

The three most recognised global symbols are Coca-Cola, the cross and McDonald's golden arches. Talk about what these symbols communicate. What about other brands – what do they communicate about themselves? Advertisers are very good at getting their message across in a world of hundreds of competing voices. How good are we at communicating God's message to the world around us?

1 Nebuchadnezzar is all-powerful (v37–38). He has little regard for others' lives (v5, v12). He seems spiritually sensitive, troubled by his dream (v1). He seems dissatisfied with the wisdom of his magicians and astrologers (v8,9).

2 Get people to share what they noticed during the week and discuss if and how Christians should be different in the ways in which they seek guidance and wisdom.

3 Encourage people to tell their stories. Talk about discernment – how can we know when something is from God and when it's just our own interpretation?

4 Daniel's response demonstrated all these characteristics of God. He showed Arioch that God was trustworthy, his friends that God heard and would answer prayer, and Nebuchadnezzar that his God was powerful and in charge of the future. His thankful prayer says all these things.

5 Daniel prayed to God for wisdom. His prophetic gift was grounded in his relationship with God. He had both intimacy with God and involvement in the world around him. And it's possible that Nebuchadnezzar had heard about what Daniel and his friends had done earlier in refusing the king's food and yet being healthier than everyone else. In any case it's clear that Arioch, the commander of the king's guard, had respect for Daniel. Daniel's actions matched his words.

6 Daniel realised that God is not just the God of his people Israel; God is the God of all creation, the God of all history and the God of all people. His God has authority over this pagan king. And as a prophet he is authorised to call all those in political power to account on the basis of God's universal, creational laws of justice and righteousness.

7 Verse 2:28 is quite a good summary – there is a God in heaven who is able to reveal mysteries. Daniel is saying that behind the scenes of history, the purposes of God are being worked out. God is in control and he is sovereign.

9 Jesus said that the world would know that we are his disciples by the way that we love each other. The quality of our relationships should be a sign of the kingdom. The church needs to stand between God and the world, showing the world what God is like and what are the concerns on his heart, and bringing the world to God in prayer. The church needs to be a signpost to the kingdom – a community that reminds others of the real thing. People in your group will have different views on the issues on which the church should speak out. Encourage them to share those views and point out that people may be called to be active in different areas, but that there will probably be others in the church who feel like they do and with whom they can work.

10 Daniel spoke with wisdom and tact (2:14). He addressed Nebuchadnezzar respectfully and appropriately. His life was consistent with his words.

WORSHIP

Hand out the newspapers and get people to cut out the issues that they long for God to speak into. Stick these onto the large sheet of paper using the glue sticks. You may want to spread old newspapers under the large sheet for the painting to protect your floor or table. Then invite people to pray for these different areas, and as they do so to paint over and around the words with the gold and silver paint, as if they are painting God's words and God's perspective into the situation. You could play some worship music in the background as you do this.

SESSION 3

YOU WILL NEED

▶ Verses from the psalms written onto pieces of paper – see the worship instructions below.

TO SET THE SCENE

You could show a clip from one of the films suggested or one of your favourites. Choose a clip with lots of action to get people talking!

1 This question is important to find out the different views in your group. Some people may take passages like this literally and expect to be able to tell what will happen in the future or link them to events in history that would have been in the future to Daniel. Others will usually avoid reading passages like this because they are too difficult to understand. Make space for a range of views.

2 Daniel's vision also included four kingdoms with God's kingdom ultimately being established over all the others.

3 The two extremes are either to try and interpret every tiny detail, linking it to specific current events and using these passages to predict future events, or to ignore these passages altogether because they are too difficult to understand. Overall passages like this are meant to give us hope – to show that God is in control and will remain so.

You could ask people to pick out key verses that seem to sum up Daniel's vision. God will ultimately overcome the evil forces of the day. Daniel's vision proclaims the future victory of God so that he can find hope in his present experience.

4 Share these passages out among your group, asking people to read and discuss them and to report back to the rest of your group. Both Peter and Paul refer to Old Testament prophecies that were fulfilled in Jesus. Philip was given a specific word that directed him to what God wanted him to do. Peter and John describe the future in a way that gives hope and courage to God's people in the circumstances they face. Predictive prophecy was part and parcel of early church life.

5 God is described as a shepherd (Ps. 23); a warrior (Ex. 15:3); a Rock (Deut. 32:4); and a fortress (Ps. 46:7).

6 To take the metaphor of God as a Rock as an example – this tells us that God is strong, dependable, enduring, a safe place, he cannot be moved or shaken. But God is not like a rock in that he is a person not an object; he can move and respond; he is not tied to one place and time.

7 Getting people in your group to verbalise this will show what they have learned through the session. You could get people to work in twos, perhaps doing a role-play, where one person plays the role of the non-Christian. See if your group can come up with creative suggestions for how this passage from Daniel might come up in conversation!

WORSHIP

Write these references onto pieces of paper to hand out to people who don't know the psalms very well and won't feel confident finding verses on their own. To avoid people being embarrassed, you could hand out slips to everyone and invite them to look up their favourite verses or the ones on the slips.

Psalm 18:1–3; Psalm 24:1–10; Psalm 27:1–3; Psalm 34:1–7; Psalm 46:1–3; Psalm 48; Psalm 63:1–5; Psalm 66:1–7.

Leaders' Guide

YOU WILL NEED

- Some play dough – enough for everyone to have a small lump.
- A marshmallow, a toy truck, a piece of ribbon or string to lie out on a table or on the floor, small counters as found in many games – one for each person.
- Information about persecuted Christians – see instructions for worship below.
- An inkpad – one that is used for ink stamps.

TO SET THE SCENE

Give everyone a small piece of play dough and invite them to make a shape or object that represents how their week has been. This is a creative way to get people to talk about how they are. Link to the theme of this week's reading – having put your play dough under pressure, we're now going to look at what happens when faith is put under pressure.

1   Lie out the piece of string on a table or on the floor. At one end put a marsh-mallow; at the other put the toy truck. This represents a pressure continuum – from the pressure exerted by a marshmallow (i.e. not very much!) to the pressure exerted by a ten-ton truck. Invite people to take a counter and put it on the line at the place corresponding to how much pressure their faith has come under in their lives. Ask them to explain why they have put their counter there. Our faith comes under pressure when we face difficulties – a relationship going wrong, death or illness, difficulties at work and so on.

2   The issue is worship. Shadrach, Meshach and Abednego can cope with captivity in a different culture, they can deal with being in exile, but they will not give up on the worship of their God. Nebuchadnezzar is challenging the second commandment 'You shall not make for yourself an idol... You shall not bow down to them or worship them' (Ex. 20:4–6).

3   Useful questions to ask are: What do people make sacrifices for? What do they spend their time and money on? What are people's goals and ambitions? Some people worship money and status; some pursue the perfect body; for some an ideal family is their ultimate goal and the thing they will make sacrifices for; for others, power is their god; some will seek celebrity.

4   Their statement shows great faith in God, but it is also realistic. They don't know how God will choose to answer their prayers, but they know they can't dictate to him what he should do. He is still God whether he saves them or not.

5   Shadrach, Meshach and Abednego have to go through their trial rather than being rescued from it. We don't develop godly character by escaping difficulties!

6   Some people may have painful stories to tell. Make sure they are heard with respect.

7   We would become more informed about the situations in which Christians are persecuted. We would pray more regularly instead of once a year on an ear-marked Sunday. We might get involved personally by supporting agencies working with the persecuted church.

8   Make space to hear different opinions.

9   He enters the furnace with them, coming alongside them in their ordeal. He brings them through their trial in an amazing way.

10 Nebuchadnezzar has to acknowledge that the God of these Jewish exiles is THE God. He offers praise to God and affirms Shadrach, Meshach and Abednego for disobeying his own command. He goes a bit overboard in his enthusiasm (v29)!

WORSHIP

Find out about persecuted Christians. Your church leader or someone in your church may be able to give you information. Or visit the websites of these organisations below and contact them for more information. Gather some stories that people can pray about – not so many that you overwhelm people. Have an inkpad and invite people to leave their fingerprints beside the pictures and stories for people for whom they pray during this worship time. When we apply pressure to the inkpad, we can produce a print that displays our uniqueness and reminds us that we are created by God. Putting our fingerprints beside others as we pray affirms their uniqueness too and shows that we stand alongside them.

Release International   www.releaseinternational.org

Voice of the Martyrs   www.persecution.com

Christian Solidarity Worldwide   www.csw.org.uk

SESSION 5

YOU WILL NEED

▶ CD of instrumental worship music and a CD player.
▶ Candle and matches.

TO SET THE SCENE

We tend to be creatures of habit and a lot of that is built around the things we do regularly – such as going to work, taking children to school and so on. But it's interesting to think about how we get into those routines, and consequently how we might start up new routines.

1 There are lots of parallels:

▶ The issue at stake is worship (3:5, 6:7)
▶ Daniel and his friends disobey the orders of the king (3:18, 6:10)
▶ Daniel and his friends are both denounced by their colleagues (3:12, 6:12)
▶ They are sentenced to death (3:20, 6:16)
▶ The angel of the Lord comes to them (3:25, 6:22)
▶ They emerge totally unharmed (3:27, 6:23)
▶ Some of the king's people are killed instead (3:22, 6:24)
▶ Both kings acknowledge that God really is God (3:28, 6:26)
▶ Both try to order everyone to worship the one true God (3:29, 6:26)

The subtle difference is that Shadrach, Meshach and Abednego were punished for refusing to worship idols; Daniel was punished for refusing to stop worshipping the one true God.

2 Daniel's practice of prayer was regular and predictable. His faith was public and not hidden from those around him who worshipped other gods. His faith was more important to him than his own life.

3 People may come up with all kind of ideas here – and time pressure is bound to be one of them. Without being heavy-handed, see if one of the issues is the amount of time spent on amusements and entertainment – watching TV, for instance! Finding somewhere quiet may be a real issue too – encourage people to share how they overcome these issues.

4 Encourage people to share their views which may be very different. Remind people to talk in general terms rather than talking about specific people or churches. I think the two most dangerous seductions are the cult of celebrity and the pursuit of wealth and comfort.

5   People will have different views on this question too. Make space for lots of different voices to be heard.

6, 7   Try not to let this discussion get competitive! Remind people that in different seasons of our lives we will have different amounts of time and space for prayer. What is important is that individuals find a practice that suits them and helps their relationship with God to grow.

8   Darius, the king who had commanded that no one prayed to anyone except him, defies his own decree and prays to Daniel's God. An interesting question to think about is whose prayer did God answer when he kept Daniel safe – Darius's or Daniel's?

9   Encourage people to be imaginative and dream first, then talk about what's practical later. If we are too quick to say 'that won't work' or 'I haven't got time for that' we can miss out on new things that God might want to do in us.

WORSHIP

Read the Steve McVey quote and explain that you will have a time of quiet prayer. Light the candle to represent God's presence among you. You may like to play some instrumental worship music quietly in the background to help people relax. Invite people to make themselves comfortable and to close their eyes; they may like to hold their hands open in their laps. Invite people to become aware of their breathing – to breathe out stress and the things on their mind; to breathe in the presence of God.

LEADERS' GUIDE

Read these words slowly, allowing time for people to reflect on what is being said.

This is holy space
God is here – you are welcome
This is your space to be with God
And God's space to be with you
Make yourself at home
Be yourself
Be real
There's no rush
Let God love you
Let God know you
Let God heal you
Let God speak to you
Receive from God
Commune with God
Feed on God

From The Labyrinth Meditations CD © Proost. Used with permission.

Allow some time for silence after this reading. When it is time to finish, invite people to say the grace together or close with a time of prayer.

SESSION 6

YOU WILL NEED

▶ Paper and pens for the worship time.

TO SET THE SCENE

Look out for lists of the world's most powerful men or women that are published from time to time to use as a discussion starter. A search on a newspaper site such as the Guardian www.guardian.co.uk should help you locate a recent list.

As part of this conversation talk about what power is. How do people get power? Why do they want power?

1   Nebuchadnezzar has seen Daniel interpret his dream and acknowledged that Daniel's God was the God of gods and the Lord of kings (2:47). He saw Shadrach, Meshach and Abednego survive the fiery furnace, and tried to make everyone worship God as a result (3:28–29). It seems amazing that he should have had those encounters and yet still not worship God. Perhaps he is just too proud.

2   Nebuchadnezzar has besieged Jerusalem and taken its people into exile (1:1,2). He has sentenced people to death (2:13 and 3:15) and ordered others to bow down and worship a huge statue of himself (3:4–6). Daniel acknowledges Nebuchadnezzar's power (2:37, 4:22). In contrast Daniel has little power – he is captive in a foreign court far from home. He has influence because of his relationship with God and his ability to interpret dreams and make wise decisions, but he has little power to do what he wants.

3   God is mightier even than this mighty king.

4   Jesus said that Pilate only had power because God had given it to him. When we look at the world's leaders and the power that God has given them, we might struggle with the question of why he chooses to allow them so much power. Let people discuss the issues freely – this is not an easy question to answer.

5 Share the passages between people in the group. Ask them to look them up and report back to the rest of the group.

Acts 1:8 – the disciples are told to stay in the city until they are clothed with power from on high.

1 John 4:4 – we have Christ's power in us which is greater than any power in the world.

Matthew 17:20 – power is linked to faith. With only the tiniest amount of faith, we can do great things in God's power.

1 Corinthians 2:1–5 – the power that is accessed by faith contrasts strongly with the worldly power that comes from human strength and achievement.

6 Again, give these passages to individuals or pairs in your group and ask them to read them and report back.

John 13:1–5 – he washed the disciples feet.

Matthew 20:20–28 – he told his disciples not to lord it over each other.

Matthew 10:1–10 – He gave power away to his disciples.

Matthew 21:12–17 – He used his power responsibly.

Matthew 26:47–56 – He could have used his power to avoid arrest and death, but he chose not to.

7 The church has tended to follow the dominant understanding of leadership that Nebuchadnezzar followed – that leadership automatically carries power and privilege. Some will argue that in the past the church has abused its power in trying to make people convert or conform to its ideals in many places around the world. Others may have come out of churches where power was abused – be sensitive to this.

8 Mission would be done with a servant heart, finding out what people's needs are, living among them rather than imposing our solutions from outside.

9 There is scope for lots of discussion here! Remind people to talk in general terms rather than about individuals. We are all part of the church so when we say 'the church ought to do this...' we are talking about ourselves.

WORSHIP

All of us have power of one sort or another – whether that's power in the work-place, or at home over our family, or in our circle of friends. Invite people to choose a symbol of that power – a mobile phone or keys could represent work, for exam-ple. If they don't have that thing with them they can draw it on the paper available. You could get people to talk about what they have drawn and why. Invite people to pray, and then to take back their symbols of power, realising that they are a gift from God and to be used responsibly.

SESSION 7

YOU WILL NEED

▶ Someone who can lead a song of worship and praise during the worship, plus songbooks for the words.

TO SET THE SCENE

If people have not had a chance to meet up with others in the week, get them to talk about older Christians that they know.

1 Both rulers set themselves up as all-powerful and refuse to worship God even though they know about him. Both are confronted with God's greater power. Nebuchadnezzar is a powerful dictator bur he is not beyond redemption. He experiences some kind of conversion. Belshazzar is arrogant and corrupt and is slain for it.

2 Using the goblets shows his disdain for God. He commits blasphemy by using something sacred to God for another purpose and combines it with idolatry by using the goblets to drink to his powerless gods.

3 Everyone will have to answer to God; no one is too powerful or too depraved.

4 We just don't know, but there's a lot more of Daniel's life outside of the book than there is in it. The rest of Daniel's life was probably very ordinary – plenty of hard work in helping to run the country. The point is that he was faithful throughout his life, not just in the dramatic moments.

5 Encourage people to share their stories. Some may find it easier if you interview them with these questions so the onus is not on them to construct a narrative. Everyone has something of value to share.

6, 7 You are asking people to make themselves vulnerable as they answer these questions. If appropriate, remind people not to talk outside of the group about what has been shared in it. Thank people for their contributions and show that you value them.

8 Daniel probably longed to go back to Jerusalem throughout his time in exile. He was holding onto God's promise that the exiles would return but we don't know if he did return. His understanding of God has been enlarged; his faith has been tested and he has remained faithful.

9 Encourage everyone to share something. It's important that people realise that it's OK to still have questions.

WORSHIP

If your group aren't very good at singing, you could play a track from a worship CD for people to listen to or even sing along to.